Sports Illustrated KIDS

BASEBALL'S ORIGIN STORY

by Matt Chandler

CAPSTONE PRESS
a capstone imprint

Published by Capstone Press, an imprint of Capstone
1710 Roe Crest Drive, North Mankato, Minnesota 56003
capstonepub.com

Copyright © 2025 by Capstone. All rights reserved. No part of this publication may be reproduced in whole or in part, or stored in a retrieval system, or transmitted in any form or by any means, electronic, mechanical, photocopying, recording, or otherwise, without written permission of the publisher.

SPORTS ILLUSTRATED KIDS is a trademark of ABG-SI LLC.
Used with permission.

Library of Congress Cataloging-in-Publication Data
Names: Chandler, Matt, author.
Title: Baseball's origin story / by Matt Chandler.
Description: North Mankato, Minnesota : Capstone Press, [2025] | Series: Sports Illustrated kids: sports origin stories | Includes bibliographical references and index. | Audience: Ages 8-11 | Audience: Grades 4-6 | Summary: "The crack of the bat! A close play at home! You love the thrill of baseball. But where and how did this heart-thumping sport begin? What were the original rules? What equipment did players use? And how has the sport changed since then? Get the answers to all your questions and more!"— Provided by publisher.
Identifiers: LCCN 2024022727 (print) | LCCN 2024022728 (ebook) | ISBN 9781669090243 (hardcover) | ISBN 9781669090199 (paperback) | ISBN 9781669090205 (pdf) | ISBN 9781669090229 (kindle edition) | ISBN 9781669090212 (epub)
Subjects: LCSH: Baseball—History—Juvenile literature.
Classification: LCC GV867.5 .C42 2025 (print) | LCC GV867.5 (ebook) | DDC 796.357—dc23/eng/20240520
LC record available at https://lccn.loc.gov/2024022727
LC ebook record available at https://lccn.loc.gov/2024022728

Editorial Credits
Editor: Mandy Robbins; Designer: Elyse White; Media Researcher: Jo Miller; Production Specialist: Tori Abraham

Image Credits
Alamy: Glasshouse Images, 22, Joe Vella, 11; AP Images: Julio Cortez, 24; Getty Images: Bettmann, 9, Icon Sportswire, 15, Minnesota Historical Society, 14, Richard Drury, 16, shmackyshmack, 17; Granger, 13; Library of Congress, cover (bottom), 10; Shutterstock: Sean Pavone, 26, zieusin, cover (top); Sports Illustrated: Erick W. Rasco, 4, 18, 25, 28, John G. Zimmerman, 12, John W. McDonough, 20, V.J. Lovero, 27; Superstock: Buyenlarge, 8, Mary Evans Picture Library, 7

Any additional websites and resources referenced in this book are not maintained, authorized, or sponsored by Capstone. All product and company names are trademarks™ or registered® trademarks of their respective holders.

TABLE OF CONTENTS

INTRODUCTION
TEXAS MAGIC..........................4

CHAPTER 1
PLAY BALL!............................6

CHAPTER 2
AMERICA'S PASTIME..................10

CHAPTER 3
CHANGES TO THE GAME...............16

CHAPTER 4
**TODAY'S BASEBALL:
A BILLION-DOLLAR BUSINESS**..........22

Timeline......................... 29
Glossary......................... 30
Read More........................ 31
Internet Sites................... 31
Index............................ 32
About the Author................. 32

Words in **bold** are in the glossary.

INTRODUCTION
TEXAS MAGIC

It was the top of the ninth inning in Game 5 of the 2023 **World Series**. The Texas Rangers led the series three games to one over the Arizona Diamondbacks.

Diamondbacks closer Paul Sewald was on the mound for Arizona. His team trailed 3-0. He needed to shut down the Rangers and give his teammates one last chance to make a comeback. Texas second baseman Marcus Semien had other plans.

Rangers teammates celebrate their 2023 World Series win.

With a runner at third base, Semien stepped to the plate. Sewald left a ball up in the strike zone. Semien swung and crushed a long drive to deep left field. The ball landed six rows deep in the stands. The home run gave the Rangers a 5–0 lead! The Diamondbacks' dream was crushed. The win gave the Rangers their first World Series title in team history!

By 2023, the sport of baseball had a long and storied history. But where did it all begin? Turn the page to find out.

FACT

The New York Yankees hold the record for most World Series titles. The Bronx Bombers have played in 40 World Series and won 27 championships!

CHAPTER 1
PLAY BALL!

The National Baseball Hall of Fame is in Cooperstown, New York. It was built to honor Abner Doubleday, the man credited with inventing the game in Cooperstown in 1839. There is just one problem—Doubleday did not invent baseball. That story is a myth created more than 100 years ago.

Baseball wasn't invented by any single person. Games such as **cricket** and **rounders** were being played in England long before 1839. Many historians believe baseball grew out of a mix of those games. Baseball had been played in America as far back as 1750.

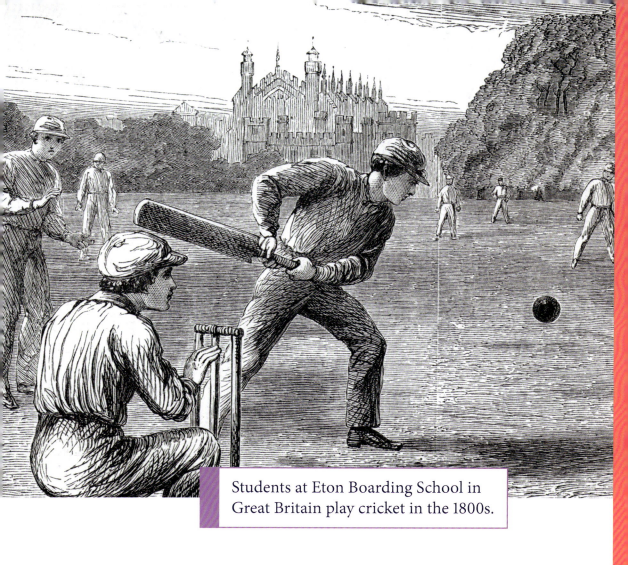

Students at Eton Boarding School in Great Britain play cricket in the 1800s.

In its early days, baseball was popular in western Massachusetts, the Philadelphia area, and upstate New York. Each region had rules that were a little bit different. The New York rules were closest to today's game.

People had been getting together to play games like baseball for many years. It wasn't until 1845 that the first official baseball team was formed. Alexander Cartwright founded the New York Knickerbocker Base Ball Club.

The club had 20 rules for the game. Rule Number 4 called for the bases to be laid out in a diamond shape. Before the Knickerbockers, baseball was often played on a rectangular field.

The Mutual Club of Manhattan faced the Atlantic Club of Brooklyn in the 1865 championship game in Hoboken, New Jersey.

Members of the Knickerbocker Base Ball Club and the Excelsior Base Ball Club, 1858

On June 19, 1846, the Knickerbockers played what is considered by many historians to be the first official baseball game. They challenged the New York Nine, a team of cricket players. The Knickerbockers lost 23–1.

FACT

In one of the earliest versions of baseball, runners did not have to stay on the basepaths. Fielders sometimes chased them all over the park trying to tag them out!

CHAPTER 2
AMERICA'S PASTIME

Baseball soon exploded in popularity. Teams formed all over the country at the club and collegiate level. This led to the development of professional baseball. In 1869, the Cincinnati Red Stockings became the first pro baseball team in America. The National League of Baseball Clubs was founded in 1876. It was made up of eight teams. The National League still exists today, though there are now 15 teams.

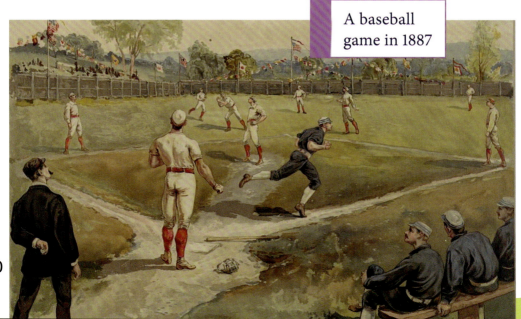

A baseball game in 1887

Willie Keeler of the New York Highlanders swings while Lou Criger of the Boston Red Sox catches in a 1908 game.

In 1901, the American League was formed to compete with the National League. The **rival** leagues agreed that their best teams should play at the end of each season to crown a champion. The World Series was born!

In 1903, the Boston Americans defeated the Pittsburgh Pirates to win the first World Series! Both original teams are still active today, though in 1908 the Americans changed their name to the Boston Red Sox.

THE NEGRO LEAGUES

Hall of Fame infielder Jackie Robinson is credited with breaking the color barrier in baseball. In 1947, Robinson was the only Black player in Major League Baseball (MLB). But he wasn't the first. He was merely the first in 60 years. Black players regularly played baseball in the 1800s. In 1887, baseball owners reached a secret **racist** pact. They agreed to no longer give contracts to Black baseball players.

Jackie Robinson playing for the Brooklyn Dodgers in 1956

1937 American Negro Leagues All-Star team, including Satchel Paige (2nd row, far right)

Instead of giving up, these talented players formed independent teams and played what competition they could find. In 1920, the Negro National League was formed. Soon, other leagues for Black players arose. The Negro Leagues were filled with superstars. Among them was pitcher Satchel Paige. Paige became the first player from the Negro Leagues to pitch in the World Series. He helped the Cleveland Indians win the title in 1948—as a 42-year-old **rookie!**

Throughout the 1950s, **integration** allowed more players from the Negro Leagues to join MLB. That led to the end of the Negro Leagues. Today, 37 players from the Negro Leagues are members of the National Baseball Hall of Fame.

WOMEN'S PROFESSIONAL BASEBALL

In 1942, more than 500 MLB players left to fight in World War II (1939–1945). Stars such as Red Sox outfielder Ted Williams and Cleveland Indians pitcher Bob Feller went from baseball heroes to military heroes.

Owners worried fans wouldn't come to games without the star players. But they thought a women's professional league might draw fans. Women had played in clubs and independent leagues for years. In 1943, the All-American Girls Professional Baseball League (AAGPBL) was born.

Shirley Jameson of the Kenosha Comets rounds a base.

The AAGPBL had stars too. Catcher May "Bonnie" Baker could throw a ball 345 feet (105 meters). Speedy Sophie Kurys stole 201 bases in a single season. Olive Little of the Rockford Peaches was the first player in the AAGPBL to throw a **no-hitter**.

At the height of its popularity, the AAGPBL drew more than 910,000 fans to its games. By 1954, the men were back from war, and MLB games were on television. Fans returned to watching MLB, and the AAGPBL shut down.

COACHING SUCCESS

No women have ever played in a major-league game. However, in 2020, Alyssa Nakken made history. She joined the San Francisco Giants as the first full-time female coach in MLB history.

Two seasons later, the Yankees hired Rachel Balkovec to manage the organization's Class-A minor-league team. In 2022, 11 women served as coaches at the minor-league or major-league level!

Rachel Balkovec

CHAPTER 3
CHANGES TO THE GAME

In 1923, MLB teams hit an average of 61 home runs for the season. In 2023, that number was 196. The biggest reasons for the power explosion are improvements in bats and balls over time. Early baseballs were often made from pieces of old shoe rubber and yarn. Every ball was a different shape and weight. Because the balls were soft, it was hard to hit them very far. Modern baseballs have rubber or cork centers. These much harder balls go farther when hit.

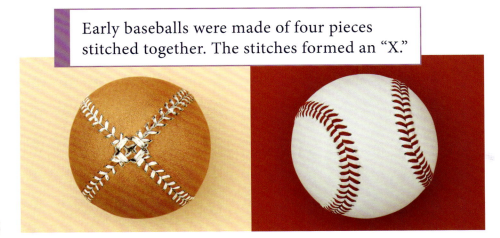

Early baseballs were made of four pieces stitched together. The stitches formed an "X."

The original baseball bats were very heavy and up to 1 foot (30.5 centimeters) longer than today's bats. They were often flat on one side, like a cricket bat. As pitchers began to throw faster, batters needed to swing faster. Lighter bats made that possible.

FROM BARE HANDS TO GLOVES

In the early days, players caught the ball with their bare hands! By the 1860s, a few players wore work gloves to protect their hands. The first glove designed for baseball was invented in the 1870s. By the 1890s, most players wore gloves. Eventually, designers added a pocket to gloves. Now they were not just for protection. They helped players catch the ball more easily. Today, there are specialty gloves for different positions on the field.

RULES OF THE GAME

The National Baseball Hall of Fame credits Knickerbockers founder Alexander Cartwright with inventing some of the rules of modern-day baseball in 1845. A revision in 1857 established more rules that remain intact today. They include that each team must have no more than nine players on the field. They also stated that the bases should be 90 feet (27 m) apart, and games would be nine innings long.

Seattle Mariner Julio Rodriguez steps up to the plate wearing a helmet that protects his face.

More rules have been added over time. Some are made to keep players safe. In 1971, a new rule required batters to wear a hard protective batting helmet. The rule expanded to base coaches after minor-league first-base coach Mike Coolbaugh was killed by a ball that hit him in the head in 2007.

THE PINE TAR GAME

In 1955, a rule was made that allowed players to add a sticky substance called pine tar up to 18 inches (46 cm) from the bottom of the bat. It helped players grip the bat better. That rule famously came into play in a 1983 game at Yankee Stadium. Kansas City's George Brett hit a go-ahead home run in the ninth inning. But Yankees Manager Billy Martin argued that Brett had pine tar too far up his bat. The umpires agreed and Brett was called out, giving the Yankees the win!

After the game, the Royals protested, and the commissioner said that Brett had not violated the "spirit of the rule." The game was resumed from that point the next time the Royals were in New York. An unhappy Billy Martin played his players out of position in protest. The Royals ended up winning the game.

Shohei Ohtani is the only pitcher who is also a designated hitter.

Other rules have been added to make the games more exciting. Pitchers are usually not good hitters. Having a spot in the lineup that is almost an automatic out makes the game less fun to watch for fans. In 1973, the American League added the "Designated Hitter (DH)" rule. The DH is a player who hits in place of the pitcher during the game. The National League adopted the DH rule in 2022.

In 1878, it took nine balls to walk a batter. Today, it takes four, and the game goes much faster. This too can make it more enjoyable for fans to watch. In 1969, the pitcher's mound was lowered from 15 to 10 inches (38 to 25 cm). That made it easier on the hitters and added more offense to the game.

In the field, teams used to be able to shift their defense and move players to the areas where a batter usually hits the ball. This defensive shift made it harder to get a base hit. Most fans love high-scoring games so, in 2023, baseball banned defensive shifts.

FACT

Major League Baseball uses as many as 300,000 baseballs each season. Each one is sewn by hand with 108 double stitches.

CHAPTER 4
TODAY'S BASEBALL: A BILLION-DOLLAR BUSINESS

Many fans consider Babe Ruth to be the greatest baseball player who ever lived. In 1927, Ruth signed a three-year contract with the New York Yankees. They paid him $70,000 per season. It was the largest contract in history at that time. If Ruth were playing today, he would be earning millions of dollars per season.

Babe Ruth, 1924

In 2024, the lowest-paid MLB player earned $740,000 per season. The highest-paid player was Los Angeles Dodgers pitcher and designated hitter Shohei Ohtani. In 2023, he signed a 10-year contract for $70 million per season! The big salaries are worth it. Major League Baseball brought in more than $10 billion in 2023.

But the majors aren't the only place baseball equals big money. **Amateur** and minor-league baseball thrives throughout the United States as well. Even kids' games can bring in big money. The Little League World Series brought $35 to $40 million into the Williamsport, Pennsylvania, region in 2023. The youth baseball event has been held there since 1947.

FACT

MLB players get perks with their contracts. Angels superstar Mike Trout has his own luxury suite at the ballpark. Former Cubs pitcher Jon Lester got the use of a private jet. Former Houston Astros pitcher Charlie Kerfeld received 37 boxes of orange Jell-O each season.

TOUGH COMPETITION

In the early 1900s, baseball was the most popular sport in America. A lot has changed since then. The growth of professional basketball, football, hockey, and soccer has given baseball some tough competition. It is now the fifth-most popular sport in America among young people.

Baltimore Orioles pitcher Dean Kremer winds up his pitch as the pitch clock counts down.

Arizona Diamondback Geraldo Perdomo steals second base during Game 1 of the 2023 World Series.

MLB has made changes to increase professional baseball's popularity. They have taken steps to shorten games to make them more exciting. In 2023, MLB added a pitch clock. It forces pitchers to pitch more quickly. The league also banned defensive shifts and increased the size of the bases in 2023. Larger bases allow more runners to reach and steal bases. More runners on base leads to more scoring and more excitement!

BASEBALL AROUND THE WORLD

There are 30 teams in Major League Baseball. The sport is also popular in other countries. Eighteen teams compete in the Mexican League. Huge crowds also watch professional baseball in Australia, the Dominican Republic, and Venezuela.

The most popular international baseball league is Nippon Professional Baseball (NPB) in Japan. More than 25 million fans combined attended NPB games in 2023. NPB had the highest average attendance per game of any professional baseball league.

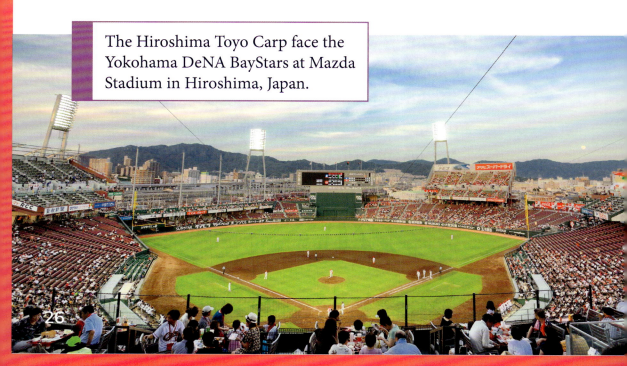

The Hiroshima Toyo Carp face the Yokohama DeNA BayStars at Mazda Stadium in Hiroshima, Japan.

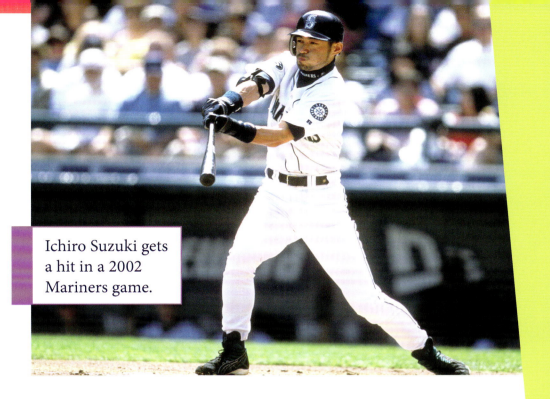

Ichiro Suzuki gets a hit in a 2002 Mariners game.

NPB has also produced some MLB superstars. Ichiro Suzuki earned 10 **Gold Gloves** and had more than 3,000 hits for the Seattle Mariners. Shohei Ohtani got his start in NPB before joining the Los Angeles Angels in 2018. Ohtani was named the American League's Most Valuable Player (MVP) in 2021 and 2023.

FACT

MLB plays international games too. In 2023, the San Diego Padres and San Francisco Giants played two games in Mexico City.

A GLOBAL GAME OF GREATNESS

Baseball is a game for anyone and everyone to love. With leagues at the youth, college, amateur, minor, and professional level, it's a game everyone can enjoy.

Major League Baseball is working to make the game faster and more exciting for fans. It is expanding its international play. Professional baseball has more women in coaching roles than ever before.

Outside the majors, baseball is booming too. A 2021 report found that about 15.6 million Americans played amateur baseball that year. Nearly 200 years after it began, it's easy to see why baseball became "America's Pastime."

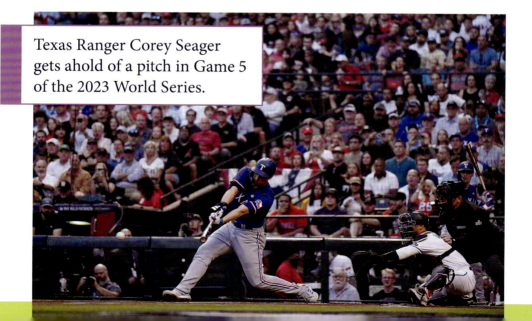

Texas Ranger Corey Seager gets ahold of a pitch in Game 5 of the 2023 World Series.

TIMELINE

1846 The first official game is played between the New York Knickerbockers and a team of cricket players.

1866 The first women's baseball team is formed at Vassar College in New York.

1884 Moses Fleetwood Walker becomes the first Black player in Major League Baseball.

1903 The Boston Americans and the Pittsburgh Pirates play in the first World Series.

1907 Alta Weiss becomes the first woman to play professional baseball.

1933 Baseball's first All-Star Game is played in Chicago.

1947 Jackie Robinson breaks the color barrier, becoming the first Black player in modern MLB history.

1956 Don Larsen of the Yankees pitches a perfect game in the World Series.

1973 The designated hitter rule is established.

1991 At age 44, Nolan Ryan of the Texas Rangers becomes the oldest player to throw a no-hitter.

2007 Barry Bonds sets the home run record at 762.

2023 MLB adopts new rules to make the game more exciting and move more quickly.

GLOSSARY

amateur (AM-uh-chur)—describes a sports league in which athletes are not professional players

cricket (KRI-kuht)—an outdoor bat-and-ball game that is similar to baseball

Gold Glove (GOHLD GLUHV)—an award honoring the best fielder at each position in both the National and American leagues

integration (in-tuh-GRAY-shuhn)—the practice of including people of all races

no-hitter (NO-HIT-ur)—a game in which one team doesn't allow the other team to get a hit

racist (RAY-sist)—describes actions or policies that treat someone unfairly due to race

rival (RYE-vuhl)—a person or group that competes with another

rookie (RUH-kee)—a first-year player

rounders (ROWN-duhrs)—an English game that is played with a ball and bat and that somewhat resembles baseball

World Series (WURLD SIHR-eez)—a group of games in which the best teams in the American League and National League play against each other

READ MORE

Berglund, Bruce. *Baseball Goats: The Greatest Athletes of All Time.* North Mankato, MN: Capstone, 2022.

Burrell, Dean. *Baseball Biographies for Kids: Stories of Baseball's Most Inspiring Players.* Oakland, CA: Callisto Kids, 2024.

Chandler, Matt. *Baseball's Greatest Walk-Offs and Other Crunch-Time Heroics.* North Mankato, MN: Capstone, 2021.

INTERNET SITES

Aaron Judge ALL RISE Foundation
Aaronjudgeallrisefoundation.org

Baseball: A Timeline
pbs.org/kenburns/baseball/timeline

History of Baseball in the United States Facts for Kids
kids.kiddle.co/History_of_baseball_in_the_United_States

INDEX

All-American Girls Professional Baseball League (AAGPBL), 14–15
American League, 11, 20, 27

Balkovec, Rachel, 15

Cartwright, Alexander, 8, 18
cricket, 6, 7, 9, 17, 29

Little League World Series, 23

Major League Baseball (MLB), 12, 13, 14, 15, 16, 21, 23, 25, 26, 27, 28, 29

Mexican League, 26
Most Valuable Player (MVP), 27

Nakken, Alyssa, 15
National Baseball Hall of Fame, 6, 12, 13, 18
National League, 10, 11, 20
Negro Leagues, 12–13
New York Knickerbockers, 8, 9, 18, 29
New York Yankees, 5, 15, 19, 22, 29
Nippon Professional Baseball (NPB), 26, 27

Ohtani, Shohei, 20, 23, 27

Paige, Satchel, 13
pitch clock, 24, 25

Robinson, Jackie, 12, 29
rounders, 6
rules, 7, 8, 18, 19, 20–21, 29
Ruth, Babe, 22

Semien, Marcus, 4, 5
Sewald, Paul, 4, 5

World Series, 4, 5, 11, 13, 25, 28, 29

ABOUT THE AUTHOR

Matt Chandler is the author of more than 85 books for children, including *Side-by-Side Baseball Stars*, which won the 2015 Outstanding Children's Book Award from the American Society of Journalists and Authors. Matt lives in New York with his wife, Amber, and his children, Zoey and Oliver. www.mattchandlerwriting.com